D0564138

This journal belongs to

Harry Davis

Merry Christmas my friend,

I am so blessed to know a missionary to India! I'm also ~~so~~ so thankful to call you friend. I pray this year finds your faith stronger than you can imagine as you experience what Franklin Graham calls "God Room" (you'll find it in a couple of pages). It is glorious to serve our Lord together.

Love in Christ,
Nick

GO INTO ALL THE WORLD
A MISSION JOURNAL

© 2009 Ellie Claire Gift and Paper Corp. | www.ellieclaire.com

Compiled by Joanie Garborg
Cover and interior design by Kirk DouPonce of DogEared Design | www.DogEaredDesign.com

All rights reserved.
No part of this book may be reproduced in any form without permission in writing from the publisher.

Scripture references are from the following sources: The Holy Bible, New International Version® NIV®. © 1973, 1978, 1984 by International Bible Society. Used by permission of Zondervan. The New King James Version (NKJV). Copyright © 1982 by Thomas Nelson, Inc. Used by permission. The New American Standard Bible® (NASB), Copyright © 1960, 1962, 1963, 1968, 1971, 1972, 1973, 1975, 1977, 1995 by The Lockman Foundation. Used by permission. The Holy Bible, New Living Translation, (NLT). Copyright 1996, 2004. Used by permission of Tyndale House Publishers, Inc., Wheaton, Illinois. *The Living Bible* (TLB) copyright © 1971. Used by permission of Tyndale House Publishers, Inc., Carol Stream, Illinois 60188. *The Message* © 1993, 1994, 1995, 1996, 2000, 2001, 2002. Used by permission of NavPress Publishing Group. All rights reserved.

Excluding Scripture verses and divine pronouns, in some quotations references to men and masculine pronouns have been replaced with gender-neutral references.

ISBN 978-1-934770-68-9

Printed in China

Mark 16:15

GO INTO ALL THE WORLD

A MISSION JOURNAL

...inspired by life

Jesus said to him,

"If you can believe, all things are

possible to him who believes....

With men it is impossible, but

not with God; for with God

all things are possible."

MARK 9:23; 10:27 NKJV

"God Room"

by Franklin Graham

President and CEO of Samaritan's Purse and the Billy Graham Evangelistic Association

When I was 23, Dr. Bob Pierce, founder of Samaritan's Purse, invited me to join him on a six-week mission to Asia. It was during that trip that I felt God's calling to work with hurting people in areas of the world affected by war, poverty, disease, or natural disaster.

We traveled to places such as Borneo, Thailand, India, Nepal, and Iran, visiting missionaries who were serving Jesus Christ under the most challenging circumstances imaginable. Along the way, Bob taught me many things about the Christian life and ministry. Possibly the greatest lesson I learned from Bob was a principle he called "God Room." That's the phrase he coined that simply means believing God to meet a need that is bigger than your human abilities to meet.

Bob passed away in 1979, and I succeeded him as president of Samaritan's Purse. The principle of "God Room" has served me well during more than 30 years of work in international relief and evangelism. Over and over, I have seen God miraculously provide desperately needed resources through ways that seem humanly impossible.

Here's how "God Room" works: You see a need that you believe God wants to meet, but no matter what you do, you just can't bring it about. After you have exhausted all your human effort, there's still a gap. That's when you pray and leave room for God to work. You trust Him to close the gap and watch a miracle unfold by His own provision.

Bob told me, "Faith isn't required as long as you set your goal only as high as the most intelligent and expert human efforts can reach. You don't exercise faith until you have committed more than it's possible to give."

Nothing is a miracle until it reaches the place where the utmost that human effort can do still isn't enough. God has to fill that gap—that room—between what's possible and what He wants done that's impossible. That's "God Room."

GOD'S HEART FOR MISSIONS

Missions is the overflow of our delight in God because missions is the overflow of God's delight in being God.

—John Piper

12/24/09

Beverly called = 2 verses for India

Eph 6:10 -11

Psalm 91

He said to them, "Go into all the world and preach the good news to all creation...."
Then the disciples went out and preached everywhere, and the Lord worked with
them and confirmed His word by the signs that accompanied it.

MARK 16:15, 20 NIV

HIS MISSION

God's purpose...has been unfolding around the world for thousands of years....
Short-term mission, as with any kind of Christian mission, is best defined and
evaluated by how closely we align ourselves with God Himself as He pursues
the fulfillment of His mission.

–Roger Peterson
Founder, STEM Int'l

01/11/2010   The time is starting to be
a little confusing. It is 4:40PM
now German time 10:40AM Atlanta
time and 9:10PM in Kolkota India.
The team left Atlanta late B/o bad
weather in Frankfurt, Germany.
Tim & Suzanne Zech surprised us @ the
Atlanta airport - They were returning from
Florida & came by E28. Tim & Suzanne
gathered the team - and prayed over us at
the gate. What a true blessing from God -
our Florida & Bonnie.
The trip was interesting. A young lady Laura Haley
Carmichael - lives in Madrid - from Atlanta -
fainted twice. They called for a doctor & I was
able to attend her. I pray she is ds well.
We are all very tired. We are now on our
second 8 hour flight (LH750 - Seat 44 c) the

PREPARING MY HEART

What is God teaching me?

Hartley to Kolkata India -
I have just read Catie's letter, Dad's letter & 2 of
Catherine's letters. I can't describe my feelings
I am truly blessed by God with my wife, parents
and children.

God is telling me through these letters filled
with His spoken Word to let Him set the time, direction,
steps. Trust in Him. He is all sufficient - He is
the Provider - He is my Peace - He will sustain &
uphold me - His promises are true - His power
unmeasurable -

Fill me -   My God reigns
Use me   My God saves
break me / mold me   My God moves mountains
                            He is mighty to save.

Christ is Author of Salvation -

Then He said to them, "The harvest truly is great, but the laborers are few;
therefore pray the Lord of the harvest to send out laborers into His harvest."

LUKE 10:2 NKJV

Christ is best served by people who have a passion for Him. Nothing short of passion will do. A passion to give themselves to God for the glory of His name, the extension of His kingdom, the fulfillment of His will. Can He now ignite a fire in you and me so that we, in turn, will share it with others, and then work together with them to win the world?

—George Foster
International Pastor, Bethany International Ministries

01/12/2010

After about 4 hours of sleep we all gathered for breakfast @ the hotel. It was buffett — with fruit, pineapple juice, coffee, scrambled eggs & peppers (spicy) — sausage (pork - like small cuts of ham) — fried eggs - toast.

Next came our introduction to Ashish — he met us @ the breakfast — a delightful man - joyful - expressive - reminds me some of Hector.

Next came business things: money exchange, deciding on what we would try to do in the villages, sorted through several bags of medicine left by the large team of doctors (Philip). It seemed we were in slow motion much of this time —

PREPARING MY HEART

What is God teaching me?

Before we could decide on everything it was time for lunch — grilled fish (Behket) and a delicious bread — almost like a thin pizza crust — grilled —

Next off on what is hard to describe if you have never been in a cab — in Kolkata — They drive on the opposite side of the road — no lane markings — and constant horn blowing — The people walk in the streets There are numerous bicycles, rickshaws, motorbikes and buses — with a few very old Fords.

We went to Mother Teresa's "motherhouse" and museum. She was a great and faithful servant. She mentions Jesus and her love for Him in every prayer, letter and statement. It is humbling to see

For Christ's love compels us, because we are convinced that one died for all, and therefore all died. And He died for all, that those who live should no longer live for themselves but for Him who died for them and was raised again.

2 CORINTHIANS 5:14-15 NIV

ALL ABOUT HIM

We make life so much more complicated when our approach to life is "all about me".... Life vastly simplifies and satisfaction greatly amplifies when we begin to realize our awesome roles. God is God. Frankly, it's all about Him. Thank goodness, He is the center of the universe.

—Beth Moore

The pictures of her kneeling down beside a malnourished, poverty stricken human being — holding their hand, cradling their head, rocking the children. She gave all of herself to that calling — and gave all the credit & glory to Jesus.

We next visited the orphanage —

I have a hard time dealing with these children. I long to hold each one but I seem so distant or mechanical with them. I know it is a heart issue but I don't know exactly what it is!

I prayed silently for God to give me a heart compassion and not just a head compassion for these children.

What is God teaching me?

Our next stop was The William Carey Baptist Church - founded by William Carey and Ward and Marchman in 1809. I really enjoyed walking/in that building & standing behind the original pulpit. His biography was such an inspiration - His humility & true love of Christ - it is hard to remember ever reading of such a person and his faith outside of The Bible characters -

Next was shopping - there were literally thousands of people in the streets, sidewalks and stores. Outside vendors & shops - multiple traveling street vendors (z tunkets)

It was certainly not like Guatemala

He is the image of the invisible God, the firstborn over all creation. For by Him all things were created: things in heaven and on earth, visible and invisible, whether thrones or powers or rulers or authorities; all things were created by Him and for Him.

COLOSSIANS 1:15-16 NIV

NUMBER ONE PRIORITY

You can't pour out unless God pours in. Go deep with God, making your relationship with Jesus your number one priority. Develop a hunger for God's Word. Know it deeply and study it daily. Spend time just being with God through His Word.

01/13/010 I finally slept - about 8 hours.
Today after breakfast we met for
devotions - led by Rob
        1 Chron 21:1
        2 Sam 24:1
Both verses tell the story of David's
disobedience in taking a census.
The point today was that Satan is God's
devil - God is omnipotent & sovereign -
He incited David thru His agent Satan
Satan never acts outside of God's control or
purpose.
        Christ is victorious over Satan by
conquering death - raised from the dead
in power -
        Col 2:15 - Christ triumphed over
Satan
How important that was - for our next
stop was the temple of _____
goddess of wrath who must be appeased

What is God teaching me?

by blood sacrifice (goats). I can not describe
the site of the crowds —
Their anxiety — the stress — the fear — the
darkness —
Such lost and hurting people — crowding
pushing & shoving to get into the courtyard —
then thru a line into the temple —
to walk by this evil — drunk — satanic idol —
pushed & shoved — and the entire time the
priests asking for money —

So dark
So depraved
So lost hopeless,
Compassion God did give for these people —
These who are blinded, living in
darkness — doomed for eternal hell
without Christ.

The love of God has been poured out within our hearts
through the Holy Spirit who was given to us.
ROMANS 5:5 NASB

HIS PARTNERS IN PRAYER

Mighty prayer—this is the one great spiritual force that will enable the Lord Jesus Christ to enter into full possession of His kingdom, and secure for Him... the uttermost part of the earth for His possession.... A person who can pray is the mightiest instrument Christ has in this world.

—E. M. Bounds

Less Then a block away stood Mother Teresa's home for the dest. fate and dying. Such a Contrast - such love beeng poored out on these pooret of poor.

Back to The hotel - to pack - check out -
ride to The train station - we stopped @
KFC - yes KFC - in Kolkata - to pick up
a meal. That is when it hit may -
Vomiting & diarrhea - persistent -
We went on to The train station - what a site -
What a mass of people -
but May was unable to travel - so he & I
rood back to The L. Horn Hotel - & are to
fly to Siliguri tomorrow -

This is a major stretch for me - just May & I
in Kolkata - in a taxi - Then here at the
hotel I arranged our flights out for
tomorrow - after several attempts -

The earnest prayer of a righteous person has
great power and produces wonderful results.
JAMES 5:16 NLT

EVERY THOUGHT CAPTIVE

Spiritual warfare often means coming to grips with what we are thinking and weighing it against the truth of the Word of God. You will be able to combat lies of the Enemy when you have God's Word hidden in your heart. This is key to fighting the good fight and keeping the faith.

God has placed me in a very difficult place. I am totally in His care - as always - but now I am releasing my fears onto Him - be anxious for nothing - cast all my anxieties on Him -

He is my Rock & Salvation - He will keep me. These verses I am repeating over & over - For He is good - He is the Covenant keeping God - His promises are true. Jesus has the right to all of His Father's promises - I live by God's grace alone - These same promises - Not by right but by grace - Through faith in Jesus Christ -

PREPARING MY HEART

What is God teaching me?

Truthfully - I do not know how to even
date this entry. It is 2:52 PM ~~01/17~~ 01/19/010
I have not been able to write - the
morning of the 14th I got sick - diarhea -
nausea - fever -

May 1 I got up - drank water - rode a taxi
to the airport a ~~Siliguri~~ Kolkata

That ride during the day - was very eye
opening - just watching out the window
To see the abject poverty - the filth -
the unbelievable - indescribable
darkness - the masses of people - it is
impossible to describe - to put in print
what my mind & eyes saw.

I could not take pictures because of

> Fix your thoughts on what is true, and honorable, and right, and pure, and lovely,
> and admirable. Think about things that are excellent and worthy of praise.
> PHILIPPIANS 4:8 NLT

Praise God for this Verse!

Work heartily, as Christ's servants

doing what God wants you to do.

And work with a smile on your face,

always keeping in mind that no matter

who happens to be giving the orders,

you're really serving God.

EPHESIANS 6:7 THE MESSAGE

All Smiles
by Marilyn Jansen

In meetings about our short-term mission trip to Poland, I was assured that all I had to do was pitch in a helping hand, smile, and keep a joyful spirit. No actual "ministering" would be necessary. How hard could that be?

Harder than I thought. When we got off the plane, we discovered that the Polish people were a bit suspicious of our motives. With a history of political unrest and social uncertainty, the Poles we met just wanted to know, "What do you want from us?" And thanks to an earlier visit from a group that wasn't quite honest, the people were convinced that we were either going to steal their children or demand payment for work done. They just did not trust us. Keeping a joyful spirit when people are scowling at you isn't so easy.

I conducted a volleyball clinic in the park to help advertise the church. It was fun. The children were excited to participate. The adults, however, weren't so sure. They hid behind the trees and occasionally popped their heads out to check on what we were doing. It was like being watched by lopsided jack-in-the-boxes.

For a week we held clinics, organized open picnics in the park, made balloon animals, and offered food and entertainment at the church. Most of all we smiled, explored the town and culture, and tried to erase suspicion. We were generating interest, but not much trust. I was feeling like a failure.

On one of our last days in Wolczyn, we had a dinner at the church. One of the church members pulled me aside and said, "My mother-in-law saw you today." My first thought was, *Oh no! What did I do?* "You spoke to her in Polish, smiled, and let her go in the door before you. She will try our church now."

A smile. Reaching the world can be as simple as that. Go. Help. Smile. Now that is true "ministering."

WHATEVER IT TAKES

Develop a flexible attitude, a joyful willingness to do whatever it takes.
Without flexibility you could end up returning home disappointed and unfulfilled.
Recognize that things won't always go your way. Flexibility is simply saying,
"Your will be done, Lord, not mine."

cont. The speed of the taxi - the jerking &
weaving - but part of the problem
was just - all I could do was stare -
& weep inside for these people - all
made in the image of God - all human -
but - no hope. each day an existence - a
struggle I have never experienced - just to
live. The darkness is thick & black even in the
day light.
   I remember the masses @ the temple -
pushing, shoving, shouting - just to see -
just to glimpse a hideous idol - that
is made of hands - that can not
help them - that offers no hope -
only bondage -
I do hope someone in our group have made
pictures - but I pray God will not allow
these mental pictures to fade with time
or b/o indifference

What is God teaching me?

Siliguri domestic airport was a challenge. May and I sat on the floor for 1½ hours watching the wrong posting board. If we had not asked we could have missed the flight. We rushed thru security - when I got to the gate they were looking for us - when I went to board - I found I had lost my boarding pass. A quiet, gentle Indian man - a representative of Jet Air walked me back to the security line - where my pass was lying on the floor in front of the carry on table. As we hurried back to the gate - I apologized profusely. He quietly replied that in India they had a saying that one never does something wrong the first time - one just

Our Father in heaven, hallowed be Your name. Your kingdom come.
Your will be done on earth as it is in heaven.
MATTHEW 6:9-10 NKJV

FROM COVER TO COVER

The Bible is not the basis of missions; missions is the basis of the Bible. The difference between missions being one of many topics in the Bible, or the one theme of the Bible, is a pretty important question. The stories *in the Bible* are great, but the story of *the Bible* is even more important.

—Ralph Winter
Founder, Frontier Mission Fellowship

does it better the second time.

The plane was clean & Modern—

The flight was without incident.

(I am not sure if I should write an account of my first introduction to the standard Indian toilet—in the airport @ Siliguri. I had no choice to wait—it is one you squat over & pray you don't slip or fall—enough said)

Christa & Matthew met us in Siliguri & we went to the hotel.

Unknown to us was the fact the rest of the team with the exception of Rob became very ill on the train ride with the

Same vomiting and diarrhea. It must has been a miserable ride from Kolkata to Siliguri.

When we arrived at the hotel everyone was down except Rds. We all crashed that nite - on hard beds & cold rooms - thankfully Christa & Matthew had gone & purchased blankets for us.

Our day for planning & organizing for our health camps, children's ministry & evangelism evaporated into the nite with many hurting bodies.

Friday 15th

Things were better - but still I had diarrhea & a very upset stomach - sips of water & bits of crackers

God told Abram: "Leave your country, your family, and your father's home for a land that I will show you.... You'll be a blessing."

GENESIS 12:1-2 THE MESSAGE

CROSS-CULTURAL MINISTRY

Go as a learner, a teachable newcomer. Being a cross-cultural minister means you're working blind and need someone to interpret the context for you. Only as you embrace and appreciate the culture can you share in a culturally relevant way. Jesus identified with us, and we must do the same where we serve.

were my only meal for over 36 hours.
We were able to get everyone together & up finally leaving Seliguri in the afternoon.
We were to be at a village today but that did not happen.

The ride from Seliguri to Coch Bear (Cooch be har) could never be put into words. It made the rides in Guatemala look like a wheelchair parade. There were times when I feared for our lives — when I prayed hard just to live thru this. It was a 5 hour trip — much of it @ nite over horrible roads crowded with bikes & rickshaws with no lights — trucks & buses & cars & motorcycles — and people just walking on the road.

PREPARING MY HEART

What is God teaching me?

The team seemed down on arrival at our hostel - it was a day we were to be in a village - and we were all still weak - nauseated & tired -

The letters from Catherine were like a life raft in a sea - She is such and encouragement - the words or Scripture - The names of God - The different banners for each day - a life line to the reality of God's Word Which is Truth - and His promises -

I have found it so hard to pray - all I could do was read scripture

For you know the grace of our Lord Jesus Christ, that though He was rich, yet for your sake He became poor, so that you through His poverty might become rich.
2 CORINTHIANS 8:9 NASB

BLESSED TO BLESS

God never intended for us to be mere recipients of His love; He calls us to share it with others. We are not to be reservoirs, but channels by which His love can reach the world. When He pours out His love into our hearts by the Holy Spirit, He wants us to leak like a sieve.... The whole point of being blessed is to pass the blessing on to others.

—George Foster
International Pastor, Bethany International Ministries

Jan 16th - We all felt better - actually ate some toast - still very weak & dehydrated but better. We met for prayer - & encouragement This day we would be in a village !!!
We drove out of town - finally down a narrow dirt road to the village - mostly bamboo huts - crowded together - behind the village were large rice fields - with cows, goats roaming - The rice already harvested. There was not any time to sight see or explore - There was a crowd gathered @ the 2 room school - concrete walls - tin roof - not lights or electricity. Our plan was to hold a health camp to teach about safe water, washing hands & food preparation. How to treat

What is God teaching me?

diarrhea & dehydration — ORS packet of
home made solution ( )
How to recognize fever and how to treat
fever especeally in Children.
Steve, Annette & I were to conduct the clinic.
Rob, May, Gary & Karen were to do a children's
ministry — c games, songs, puppetts to show
the creation story & then to share the gospel.
The children's ministry went well —
The health camp — Annette was excellent —
telling the information in story form & very
animated — My part was a flop...!! But then
The people became restless. They expected a
health clinic — We were not prepared. Praise God
we did bring some medicines That the
team of doctors had left from the

I have come that they may have life, and that they may have it more abundantly.
JOHN 10:10 NKJV

BY FAITH...
Christ wants not nibblers of the possible, but grabbers of the impossible.
—C. T. Studd
English missionary to China, India, and Africa

Bay of Bengal trip.
I set up a station — Ashish interpreted —
Annette & Steve acted out the pharmacy
with the help of interpreters.
May, Rob, Gary & Karin set up prayer stations
& prayed for those who came.
It was hard & chaotic. The people do not
know how to make a line — they crowd & push &
jump ahead & push ahead — There is no
privacy — When the door was opened to
allow 1–2 in / 8–9 would push in —

PREPARING MY HEART

What is God teaching me?

2/7/10

Last nite was the picture partz @ Max & Marti's. A great nite of fellowship & food. The team is mostly recovered — Gary is still having issues but is on a 3rd round of antibiotics

On 1/31/10 The team & spouses met with Roscoe & Margaret Brewer — to debrief. It was a hard time — I was still weak, not sleeping & stressed b/o a 2 day stay in the hospital — & a full week of work missed.

I did share my heart — & became a little more transparent & vulnerable.

Now faith is being sure of what we hope for and certain of what we do not see....
By faith we understand that the universe was formed at God's command,
so that what is seen was not made out of what was visible....
And without faith it is impossible to please God.

HEBREWS 11:1, 3, 6 NIV

I support short-term missions.... Such trips provide two distinct cultures a taste of the harmony that exists between members of the Body of Christ.

—Philip Yancey

God is sovereign

His decrees are in place

He does all things by The counsel (wisdom)
(divine, all-knowing, good, righteous)
of His will (His good pleasure - what pleases
Him & brings Him glory.)

I must know God - His attributes -

I must believe & have faith in Him -
& in His Word - His truth - His promises.

all things - by His sovereign decrees -

work together for good -

    Rom. 8:28

    Psm 121

    Psm 23

PREPARING MY HEART

What is God teaching me?

Psm 119: 11   in spite of Rob's continual
encouragement - I have not stored up
God's Word in my heart -
at night & in the darkness of those hotel
rooms - I grieved b/o my lack of stores
of His treasures in my heart -
The light in the rooms were too dim & the
print too small -
      but I did hold to what I had -

Psm 121   Psm 46: 10   Psm 118
Psm 23   Psm 86

Amazingly God has given me a renewed
hunger for His Word -
The Psalms are a delight to read &
digest -   Psm 119: 14 - 16
                Psm 119: 18
                Psm 119: 32 enlarge my heart
                Psm 119: 41

Be completely humble and gentle; be patient, bearing with one another in love.
Make every effort to keep the unity of the Spirit through the bond of peace.
There is one body and one Spirit.

EPHESIANS 4:2-4 NIV

Psm 119: 50, 55, 62   Psm 119: 103, 105, 114

Psm 119: 48, 76

Psm 119: 71, 92

Psm 119: 89-90-91

Lord, send me anywhere,

only go with me.

Lay any burden on me,

only sustain me.

Sever any ties but the tie

that binds me to Thy service

and to Thy heart.

DAVID LIVINGSTONE

I Am with You Always

David Livingstone, born in 1813, was a Scottish missionary, doctor, and explorer who helped open the heart of Africa to mssions.

Livingstone went to Africa in 1840 and married Mary Moffatt, the daughter of missionaries, in 1844. Several years later, they made the difficult decision that she would take the children back to England to be educated. During five lonely years of separation from his loved ones, his favorite verse, "Lo, I am with you always" (Matthew 28:20), was a treasured promise.

After a brief visit home, years passed before the children were old enough for Mary to return as a partner in his work. Not long after she rejoined him, malaria took her life despite his devoted medical care. Again, "Lo, I am with you always" brought him comfort.

Livingstone explored and mapped Africa's interior looking for opportunities for future missionary work. He saw that the blackest horror on the continent was the slave trade and devoted his energies to stopping the traffic in human lives. He continued on through danger, even threats on his life, certain of one thing: "Lo, I am with you always."

Not having seen a white person in five years, Livingstone looked up one day in 1871 to see Henry M. Stanley, who greeted him with the unforgettable words: "Dr. Livingstone, I presume." Stanley was a reporter for the *New York Herald* sent to see if Livingstone was still alive and bring him back to civilization. Livingstone would not return with Stanley, but forged deeper into Africa, making some of his most valuable discoveries in the following two years.

Nothing was more befitting of the life he lived than the way he died. On May 1, 1873, Livingstone was found in his tent, having died on his knees in prayer. His final moments were spent in the presence of his Lord, who had said, "Lo, I am with you always, even to the end."

DAZZLING OPPORTUNITIES

God has honored this generation as He has never honored a generation before.
He has thrown dazzling opportunities before it. He has flung wide open for
it the doors of access to all parts of His world and has laid at its feet every
possible advantage and facility.

—J. Lovell Murray

PREPARING MY HEART

What is God teaching me?

Look around at the nations; look and be amazed! For I am doing something in
your own day, something you wouldn't believe even if someone told you about it.
HABAKKUK 1:5 NLT

GOD'S SUPPLY

God's work done in God's way will never lack God's supply.

—Hudson Taylor
Missionary to China

PREPARING MY HEART

What is God teaching me?

And my God will supply all your needs according to His riches in glory in
Christ Jesus. Now to our God and Father be the glory forever and ever. Amen.
PHILIPPIANS 4:19-20 NASB

EXPECT TO SERVE

There is nothing wrong with having expectations. But an expectation must be based on the truth of God's Word.... Unrealistic expectations can cause us to be disappointed, discouraged, and even angry.... Expectations usually have their root in our desire to control our circumstances or other people. This desire is not from God.

—Howard and Bonnie Lisech

PREPARING MY HEART

What is God teaching me?

Whoever wants to become great among you must be your servant...
just as the Son of Man did not come to be served, but to serve,
and to give His life as a ransom for many.

MATTHEW 20:26-28 NIV

WORKING TOGETHER

The best that God's people have to offer is ourselves. Only when we put ourselves in direct, personal relationship with the people of God in the hard places do we begin to understand their needs and accompany them in the pilgrimage of faith.... It is no longer the rich stepping down to help the poor, but brothers and sisters in Christ stepping across to journey with one another.

—Daniel Rickett

PREPARING MY HEART

What is God teaching me?

We want to work together with you so you will be full of joy,
for it is by your own faith that you stand firm.
2 CORINTHIANS 1:24 NLT

OF GREAT VALUE

It is possible for the most obscure person in a church with a heart right toward God to exercise as much power for the evangelization of the world as those who stand in the most prominent positions.

—John R. Mott

PREPARING MY HEART

What is God teaching me?

I am God, your personal God, the Holy of Israel, your Savior. I paid a huge price for you.... *That's* how much you mean to Me! *That's* how much I love you! I'd sell off the whole world to get you back, trade the creation just for you.

ISAIAH 43:3-4 THE MESSAGE

YOUR STRENGTH

Whatever the circumstances, whatever the call, whatever the duty, whatever the price, whatever the sacrifice—His strength will be your strength in your hour of need.

—Billy Graham

PREPARING MY HEART

What is God teaching me?

What an honor for me in God's eyes! That God should be my strength! He says,
"...I'm setting you up as a light for the *nations* so that my salvation becomes *global!*"
ISAIAH 49:5-6 THE MESSAGE

LET YOUR LIGHT SHINE

It doesn't take a huge spotlight to draw attention to how great our God is.
All it takes is for one committed person to so let his or her light shine before
men, that a world lost in darkness welcomes the light.

—Gary Smalley and John Trent

PREPARING MY HEART

What is God teaching me?

Let your light shine before men in such a way that they may
see your good works, and glorify your Father who is in heaven.
MATTHEW 5:16 NASB

Therefore, as God's chosen people,

holy and dearly loved, clothe

yourselves with compassion, kindness,

humility, gentleness and patience....

Let the word of Christ

dwell in you richly.

COLOSSIANS 3:12, 16 NIV

How Do I Get Started?

by Mel Cheatham, M.D.

Humanitarian relief worker and advocate, neurosurgeon, and member of the Board of Directors of Samaritan's Purse and the Billy Graham Evangelical Association.

The most frequent comment from those going for mission service may well be, "I'm willing to do whatever work they want me to do, but don't ask me to evangelize because I don't know how to do that." In the early years of my volunteer work, I could have identified well with this feeling.

When my family and I first served a six-week mission assignment in a Christian mission hospital in South Korea, we found it difficult to share our faith, because we weren't used to doing this at home.

As we later went on several short-term mission assignments, it became increasingly apparent that the initial steps in evangelism require virtually no words. What is required is the love of Jesus Christ in your heart, and then making sure His love is always visible in your smile and your gentleness toward others. The key that unlocks the door to sharing the gospel lies in striving to be Christ-like at all times. Then His love will be reflected through your caring, compassion, courtesy, and the way you complete your assignment.

A saying attributed to St. Francis of Assisi expressed this basic tenet for sharing one's faith: "Proclaim the gospel at all times. If necessary, use words." When the love of Jesus Christ radiates from your heart and can be seen in your face and in your manner, people will warm up to you as they seek what it is that is so wonderfully different about you. At that point you can share with them the story of Jesus and His love, telling them that He is your friend and that they too can come to know Him as a friend.

As you prepare to go to the mission field, and after you arrive there, pray to be like Jesus in all you do. Sharing your faith with others will be easy if you have studied the Bible, know God's Word, and allow Him to mold you in this way.

GO OUT IN JOY

You are not here in the world for yourself. You have been sent here for others. The world is waiting for you!

—Catherine Booth

PREPARING MY HEART

What is God teaching me?

You will go out in joy and be led forth in peace; the mountains and hills
will burst into song before you, and all the trees of the field will clap their hands.

ISAIAH 55:12 NIV

YOUR ASSIGNMENT

God is at work in the world, and He wants you to join Him. This assignment is called your mission, and it is different from your ministry. Your ministry is your service to believers in the Body of Christ, while your mission is your service to unbelievers in the world. God created you for both.

—Rick Warren

PREPARING MY HEART

What is God teaching me?

Now to Him who is able to do exceedingly abundantly above all that we ask
or think, according to the power that works in us, to Him be glory
in the church by Christ Jesus to all generations, forever and ever. Amen.

EPHESIANS 3:20-21 NKJV

EXALTED IN THE NATIONS

God is pursuing with omnipotent passion a worldwide purpose of gathering joyful worshipers for Himself from every tribe and tongue and people and nation. He has an inexhaustible enthusiasm for the supremacy of His name among the nations.

—John Piper

MAXIMIZING THE MISSION

What is God doing through me?

Be still, and know that I am God;
I will be exalted among the nations,
I will be exalted in the earth.

PSALM 46:10 NIV

TIME APART

Every day I need to take time to be with the Lord in a personal, devotional way.... Sometimes we need to get away with Him to reawaken us in our love relationship—especially those of us who can become so caught up in serving God that we lose our first love.

—Anne Graham Lotz

MAXIMIZING THE MISSION

What is God doing through me?

The Lord would speak to Moses face to face, as one speaks to a friend....
One day Moses said to the Lord, "...Let me know Your ways
so I may understand You more fully and continue to enjoy Your favor."

EXODUS 33:11-13 NLT

SALT AND LIGHT

The place where God calls you to is the place where your deep gladness and the world's deep hunger meet.

—Frederick Buechner

MAXIMIZING THE MISSION

What is God doing through me?

You're here to be salt-seasoning that brings out the God-flavors of this earth.
If you lose your saltiness, how will people taste godliness?... You're here to be light,
bringing out the God-colors in the world. God is not a secret to be kept.

MATTHEW 5:13-14 THE MESSAGE

THE FOCUS OF HIS LOVE

Empathy is the ability to understand and share the feelings of others. Etiquette is the good and acceptable form of manners in a given culture. Never have a superior attitude as you compare cultures. Everyone is precious to Jesus. Each is the focus of His love.

MAXIMIZING THE MISSION

What is God doing through me?

Long before He laid down earth's foundations, He had us in mind, had settled on us
as the focus of His love, to be made whole and holy by His love.

EPHESIANS 1:4 THE MESSAGE

EARTHEN VESSELS

A changed life lived for Christ is the greatest proof to man there is a God—a God who is alive and working in frail human vessels like ourselves. It was with people like ourselves that Jesus set out to change the world—and did it.

—Carolyn Lunn

MAXIMIZING THE MISSION

What is God doing through me?

_____

_____

_____

_____

_____

_____

_____

_____

_____

_____

_____

_____

_____

_____

_____

For God, who said, "Light shall shine out of darkness," is the One
who has shone in our hearts to give the Light of the knowledge of the glory of
God in the face of Christ. But we have this treasure in earthen vessels, so that the
surpassing greatness of the power will be of God and not from ourselves.

2 CORINTHIANS 4:6–7 NASB

The poor shall eat and be satisfied....

All the ends of the world shall

remember and turn to the Lord,

and all the families of the nations

shall worship before You. For the

kingdom is the Lord's, and He rules

over the nations.

PSALM 22:26-28 NKJV

Kingdom Builders

Luis and Cathy Carrion met in a church youth group in Orlando, Florida, in 1984. They experienced their first cross-cultural outreach together to Haiti in 1986, and were forever changed by it. That short-term mission experience permanently turned the path of each of their lives toward serving God in another country.

They came back motivated to do something more. After seeing the suffering of others, a response of increased appreciation for their own blessings wasn't enough. Luis and Cathy both felt compelled to live differently. Their goals radically changed, and they wanted to live with more purpose. Instead of building a small personal kingdom here on earth, they each wanted to be part of building God's kingdom on earth and in heaven.

In 1989, stranded in Haiti during a political uprising on one of those mission trips, they discovered that their mutual interest in missions had developed into a mutual calling. They married in 1991 and four beautiful kids have come along since then.

After they were married, they continued to minister with several short-term mission teams. In 1994 their passion for building God's kingdom expanded as they traveled and visited missionaries in 14 countries.

God continued to work in their lives and lead them into missions, and five years later they accepted a teaching position at a Christian bilingual school in Honduras. Over the following two years they also led short-term teams on a part-time basis.

As much as they enjoyed those years, they longed to do more to help serve as the hands and feet of Jesus to the poor of Honduras. Luis then accepted a full-time position of managing short-term medical mission teams. On those outreaches, he finds opportunities to influence team members for the kingdom of God, challenging them to view their priorities from a new world perspective.

Cathy's mom once told her, "Why run for president when you can work for the King of kings?" What other calling could be higher than the calling to build God's eternal kingdom in this world?

THEORY INTO PRACTICE

Now that you've arrived at your destination, serving in the name of Jesus becomes more than a theory. Putting it into practice—with those you have come to minister to *and* with teammates—involves inevitable challenges and struggles. But God will give you the power to put into practice what you have learned.

MAXIMIZING THE MISSION

What is God doing through me?

Put into practice what you learned from me, what you heard and saw and realized.
Do that, and God, who makes everything work together,
will work you into His most excellent harmonies.

PHILIPPIANS 4:9 THE MESSAGE

SHARED BURDENS

Not only does the local church help lost people come to faith, it helps lonely, broken-hearted people cope with the brutality of evil in this world.... People of faith help bear the burden of those who have nowhere else to turn. Lost people get found, lonely people find community, the bereaved find comfort, the committed grow deeper and stronger in their faith.

—Bill Hybels

MAXIMIZING THE MISSION

What is God doing through me?

Stoop down and reach out to those who are oppressed.
Share their burdens, and so complete Christ's law.
GALATIANS 6:2 THE MESSAGE

TO WHAT EXTENT?

The greater the extent that you go to fulfill the Great Commission in your life, the greater extent you will see God at work in your life.

—Thom Wolf
International Director of University Institute, New Delhi

MAXIMIZING THE MISSION

What is God doing through me?

_____

_____

_____

_____

_____

_____

_____

_____

_____

_____

_____

_____

_____

For I am not ashamed of this Good News about Christ. It is the power of God
at work, saving everyone who believes.... This Good News tells us how God
makes us right in His sight. This is accomplished from start to finish by faith.

ROMANS 1:16-17 NLT

GOD SO LOVED

You can give without loving. But you cannot love without giving.

—Amy Carmichael
Missionary to India

MAXIMIZING THE MISSION

What is God doing through me?

For God so loved the world that He gave His only begotten Son,
that whoever believes in Him should not perish but have everlasting life.
JOHN 3:16 NKJV

WHERE THEY ARE

Evangelization is a process of bringing the gospel to people where they are, not where you would like them to be.... When the gospel reaches a people where they are, their response to the gospel is the church in a new place.

—Vincent Donovan
Missionary to Tanzania

MAXIMIZING THE MISSION

What is God doing through me?

And the Lord added to the church daily those who were being saved.
ACTS 2:47 NKJV

BE A TEAM PLAYER

When I get my own way, that's all I get. I don't get the opportunity to deepen a relationship, to love away the rough spots in a friend, or to grow spiritually.

—Marianne Jones

MAXIMIZING THE MISSION

What is God doing through me?

Live in harmony with each other. Let there be no divisions in the church.
Rather, be of one mind, united in thought and purpose.

1 CORINTHIANS 1:10 NLT

GAIN THE WORLD

Jesus wants us to follow Him, losing our rights and gaining the world. The choice is ours. We can hold onto our rights, remain in mediocrity, and miss out on God's greater purposes for us. Or we can give them freely back to Him for the greatest privilege of all—winning this world for the kingdom of God.

—Loren Cunningham
Founder, Youth with a Mission

MAXIMIZING THE MISSION

What is God doing through me?

If any of you wants to be My follower, you must turn from your selfish ways,
take up your cross, and follow Me.... If you give up your life for My sake
and for the sake of the Good News, you will save it.

MARK 8:34-35 NLT

We know what real love is

because Jesus gave up His life for us.

So we also ought to give up our lives

for our brothers and sisters....

Dear children, let's not merely say

that we love each other; let us show

the truth by our actions. Our actions

will show that we belong to the truth.

1 JOHN 3:16, 18-19 NLT

Living the Truth

Gladys Aylward, born in 1902 in London, was challenged as a young woman to dedicate her life to serve God. She believed she was called to China, but was turned down by the China Inland Mission when she failed their exams.

Refusing to disobey God's call, in 1930 Aylward spent her life savings on the cheapest possible passage to China. There she joined elderly missionary Mrs. Jeannie Lawson and founded The Inn of the Eight Happinesses in a remote area, sharing the gospel with those who stayed there.

After a short time working together, Mrs. Lawson died. Soon Aylward accepted the position of "foot inspector," touring the countryside to enforce a new law against foot-binding young Chinese girls. This allowed her unprecedented entry to share the story of Jesus in homes throughout the area, and many came to Christ.

In 1938 when the region was invaded by Japan, Aylward led ninety-four children to safety over the mountains, enduring conditions that devastated her health. She returned to England for medical care. But as soon as she recovered, she wanted to return to China. Denied re-entry by the Communist government, she settled in Taiwan where she served God for the remaining years of her life.

Aylward's powerful prayer life was foundational to her ministry. She understood that only through constant prayer and complete dependence upon God could the kingdom be advanced.

She not only preached the gospel—she lived it. She sacrificially did something about every injustice she witnessed: prison reform, child abuse, misogyny, and poverty. She lived like the people around her in order to make the message of the gospel accessible to them. Because of the love she poured out, the Chinese called her *Ai-weh-deh*, or "Virtuous One."

For the scores of Chinese converts, Aylward showed the truth of the gospel with her actions. Hearing the gospel proclaimed and seeing it lived out eventually won over their hearts, not one at the expense of the other.

SHINE LIKE STARS

God brings imperfect people together to perform His work on earth. He does not send angels. Angels weep over this world, but God does not use angels to accomplish His purposes. He uses burdened, broken-hearted, weeping men and women.

—David Wilkerson
Founder, Teen Challenge and Times Square Church

MAXIMIZING THE MISSION

What is God doing through me?

Do everything without complaining or arguing, so that you may become blameless
and pure, children of God without fault in a crooked and depraved generation, in
which you shine like stars in the universe as you hold out the word of life.

PHILIPPIANS 2:14-16 NIV

LIFESTYLE OF FORGIVENESS

The Bible is not only written about us but to us. In these pages we become insiders to a conversation in which God uses words to form and bless us, to teach and guide us, to forgive and save us.... We gradually (or suddenly) realize that we are insiders in the most significant action of our time as God establishes His grand rule of love and justice on this earth.

—Eugene Peterson

MAXIMIZING THE MISSION

What is God doing through me?

And forgive us our debts, as we forgive our debtors.
MATTHEW 6:12 NKJV

ENCOURAGE EACH OTHER

Encouragement is awesome. It has the capacity to lift a man's or woman's shoulders. To spark the flicker of a smile on the face of a discouraged child. To breathe fresh fire into the fading embers of a smoldering dream. To actually change the course of another human being's day, week, or life.

—Charles Swindoll

MAXIMIZING THE MISSION

What is God doing through me?

When we get together, I want to encourage you in your faith,
but I also want to be encouraged by yours.
ROMANS 1:12 NLT

GOD IS FOR YOU

Grasp the fact that God is for you—let this certainty make its impact on you in relation to what you are up against at this very moment; and you will find in thus knowing God as your sovereign protector, irrevocably committed to you in the covenant of grace, both freedom from fear and new strength for the fight.

—J. I. Packer

MAXIMIZING THE MISSION

What is God doing through me?

Be strong. Take courage. Don't be intimidated.... Because God, your God, is striding ahead of you. He's right there with you. He won't let you down; He won't leave you.

DEUTERONOMY 31:6 THE MESSAGE

ATTEMPT GREAT THINGS

Expect great things from God; attempt great things for God.

—William Carey

Missionary to India, "The father of modern missions"

MAXIMIZING THE MISSION

What is God doing through me?

For God has not given us a spirit of fear and timidity, but of power, love, and self-discipline. So never be ashamed to tell others about our Lord.

2 TIMOTHY 1:7-8 NLT

A PLENTIFUL HARVEST

Our God of grace often gives us a second chance, but there is no second chance to harvest a ripe crop.

—Kurt von Schleicher

MAXIMIZING THE MISSION

What is God doing through me?

When He saw the crowds, He had compassion on them, because they were
harassed and helpless, like sheep without a shepherd. Then He said to His disciples,
"The harvest is plentiful but the workers are few. Ask the Lord of the harvest,
therefore, to send out workers into His harvest field."

MATTHEW 9:36-38 NIV

GOD'S HANDS AND FEET

We have found there's no better way to meet the urgent physical and spiritual needs than through the local church.... These are troubled times, millions of people desperately need to hear the gospel, and church networks are usually the fastest and most effective way to reach them. We don't have time to waste.

—Franklin Graham

MAXIMIZING THE MISSION

What is God doing through me?

Upon this rock I will build my church;
and all the powers of hell shall not prevail against it.
MATTHEW 16:18 TLB

So shall My word be

that goes forth from My mouth;

it shall not return to Me void,

but it shall accomplish what I please,

and it shall prosper in the thing

for which I sent it.

ISAIAH 55:11 NKJV

Mission Accomplished

Born in England in 1761, William Carey was a shoemaker by trade, but a gifted scholar, linguist, and missionary by God's grace. Widely known as "the father of modern missions," Carey was one of God's giants in the history of evangelism.

As a Baptist preacher, he almost single-handedly overturned the indifference and hostility to missions that was prevalent among churches of all denominations. In a sermon to his colleagues, he first used the words which would become the motto of modern missions: "Expect great things from God; attempt great things for God."

He was instrumental in founding the first modern missionary society, the Baptist Missionary Society, in 1792. He influenced generations toward evangelizing the world with his publication, *Enquiry*.

In 1793 Carey was sent to India by the society he had founded. At first his wife was reluctant to sail with him, having four children including a one-year-old. Carey boarded the ship anyway, and after two returns to the dock to persuade her, she and his children accompanied him.

There were years of discouragement: no Indian convert for seven years, debt, disease, deterioration of his wife's health, and the death of a son. But by the grace and power of God, Carey continued to pursue the calling planted deep in his heart.

From the beginning, Carey's goal in India was to preach the gospel by any means. When he died in 1834 after 41 years of serving the Lord there, he had been a college professor and had founded a college at Serampore. He had seen India open its doors to missionaries and had helped banish *sati* (burning widows on the funeral pyres of their dead husbands). And God's Word had gone forth. Carey had witnessed 212,000 copies of the Scriptures translated and sent out in forty different languages among three hundred million people.

Because of Carey, God's Word went forth in power. And it continued to accomplish God's purposes long after he was gone.

OUR ACCESSIBLE GOD

The wonder of our Lord is that He is so accessible to us in the common things of our lives: the cup of water...breaking of the bread...welcoming children into our arms...fellowship over a meal...giving thanks. A simple attitude of caring, listening, and lovingly telling the truth.

—Nancie Carmichael

MAXIMIZING THE MISSION

What is God doing through me?

So let us come boldly to the throne of our gracious God.
There we will receive His mercy, and we will find
grace to help us when we need it most.

HEBREWS 4:16 NLT

MAKE DISCIPLES

The church exists for nothing else but to draw people into Christ, to make them little Christs. If they are not doing that, all the cathedrals, clergy, missions, sermons, even the Bible itself, are simply a waste of time. God became Man for no other purpose.

—C. S. Lewis

MAXIMIZING THE MISSION

What is God doing through me?

Therefore go and make disciples of all nations, baptizing them in the name of the Father and of the Son and of the Holy Spirit, and teaching them to obey everything I have commanded you. And surely I am with you always, to the very end of the age.

MATTHEW 28:19-20 NIV

CALLED AND EMPOWERED

I believe that in each generation God has called enough men and women to evangelize all the yet unreached tribes of the earth. It is not God who does not call. It is we who will not respond!

—Isabel Kuhn
Missionary to China and Thailand

MAXIMIZING THE MISSION

What is God doing through me?

But you shall receive power when the Holy Spirit has come upon you;
and you shall be witnesses to Me in Jerusalem, and in all Judea and Samaria,
and to the end of the earth.

ACTS 1:8 NKJV

SAYING GOOD-BYE

Be sure to say good-bye to special people you have met. Good-byes may be difficult for you or may seem unimportant, but they mean so very much to the people whose lives you have touched during your mission.

REFLECTING ON THE JOURNEY

How is God changing me?

Being confident of this, that He who began a good work in you
will carry it on to completion until the day of Christ Jesus.
It is right for me to feel this way about all of you, since I have you in my heart.

PHILIPPIANS 1:6-7 NIV

TRUST GOD'S HEART

Because our work is God's work, and because He is ultimately responsible for the results, He gives us the freedom to leave it, to trust Him with it.

—Sherman/Hendricks

REFLECTING ON THE JOURNEY

How is God changing me?

Trust in the Lord with all your heart and do not lean on your own understanding.
In all your ways acknowledge Him, and He will make your paths straight.
PROVERBS 3:5-6 NASB

HE HAS OVERCOME

Jesus said that He has overcome the world; not we. And He will always overcome, when we will put a matter into His hands.

—Hannah Whitall Smith

REFLECTING ON THE JOURNEY

How is God changing me?

So we don't look at the troubles we can see now; rather,
we fix our gaze on things that cannot be seen. For the things we see now
will soon be gone, but the things we cannot see will last forever.

2 CORINTHIANS 4:18 NLT

A MEANINGFUL EXPERIENCE

When we allow God the privilege of shaping our lives, we discover new depths of purpose and meaning. What a joyful thought to realize you are a chosen vessel for God—perfectly suited for His use.

—Joni Eareckson Tada

REFLECTING ON THE JOURNEY

How is God changing me?

_____

_____

_____

_____

_____

_____

_____

_____

_____

_____

_____

But you are a chosen generation, a royal priesthood, a holy nation,
His own special people, that you may proclaim the praises of Him
who called you out of darkness into His marvelous light.

1 PETER 2:9 NKJV

Jesus also said, "The Kingdom of God is like a farmer who scatters seed on the ground. Night and day, while he's asleep or awake, the seed sprouts and grows, but he does not understand how it happens."

MARK 4:26-27 NLT

God Grows the Seed

by George Foster
International Pastor, Bethany International Ministries

Herb and Ruth Billman were committed to Christ and to missions. After serving in Portugal, Africa, and Vietnam, they were called to the tiny Portuguese island colony of East Timor just north of Australia in the Pacific Ocean. Friends advised them not to go and their mission would not send them.

Still, since the call would not leave, and despite the warnings that they would not find a decent place to live or obtain visas to remain there, they gathered their four children and a minimum of belongings and landed in the capital city of Dili.

Life in Timor was more difficult than they or their friends had imagined. They lived in a shack and walked daily to the center of Dili to battle for the visa they needed to stay in the country. They were unsuccessful in all their attempts, but remained faithful and witnessed courageously to anyone who would listen.

One couple did listen. They opened their small apartment to the Billmans and began to understand the gospel story. They asked Christ into their lives and invited friends to their home for Bible studies.

After two months of fruitless attempts to obtain a visa, the Billmans had to leave Timor and return home to America. Many of their friends said, "We told you not to go." It all seemed like a wasted effort.

But their work did not end. The Timorese couple stayed true. The Bible study grew into a church and then multiplied into many more. Today there are well over 100 churches and nearly 15,000 believers who came to Christ as a result of the difficult but faithful witness of the Billmans.

The seed was sown and even though little follow-up work could be done, the multiplication was tremendous. Our job is to sow the seed, but it is God's work to grow the seed.

OBSTACLES OVERCOME

We know that He gives us every grace, every abundant grace; and though we are so weak of ourselves, this grace is able to carry us through every obstacle and difficulty.

—Elizabeth Ann Seton

REFLECTING ON THE JOURNEY

How is God changing me?

He said to me, "My grace is sufficient for you, for My power
is made perfect in weakness." Therefore I will boast all the more gladly
about my weaknesses, so that Christ's power may rest on me.
2 CORINTHIANS 12:9 NIV

THE AROMA OF CHRIST

We are all missionaries.... Wherever we go, we either bring people nearer to Christ, or we repel them from Christ.

—Eric Liddell
Olympic gold medalist, missionary to China

REFLECTING ON THE JOURNEY

How is God changing me?

But thanks be to God, who always leads us in triumphal procession
in Christ and through us spreads everywhere the fragrance
of the knowledge of Him. For we are to God the aroma of Christ
among those who are being saved and those who are perishing.

2 CORINTHIANS 2:14–15 NIV

CREATED FOR GOOD WORKS

People who feel they don't have special talents and gifts may leave the work for others. But Paul tells us that Jesus is preparing us for good works and preparing good works for us. He has an ongoing plan to use us for His kingdom work. How can I allow God to change me into who He created me to be so I can do the work He created me to do?

REFLECTING ON THE JOURNEY

How is God changing me?

For we are His workmanship, created in Christ Jesus for good works,
which God prepared beforehand that we should walk in them.
EPHESIANS 2:10 NKJV

CHANGED VALUES

He is no fool who gives up what he cannot keep to gain that which he cannot lose.

—Jim Elliot

Missionary to Ecuador, martyred in 1956

REFLECTING ON THE JOURNEY

How is God changing me?

That is why we never give up. Though our bodies are dying, our spirits are being renewed every day. For our present troubles are small and won't last very long. Yet they produce for us a glory that vastly outweighs them and will last forever!

2 CORINTHIANS 4:16-17 NLT

BE THAT PERSON

Don't ever let anyone convince you that you have no power.... All significant changes in the world start slowly, at a single time and place, with a single action. One man, one woman, one child stands up and commits to creating a better world. Their courage inspires others, who begin to stand up themselves. You can be that person.

—Jones, Haenfler, and Johnson

REFLECTING ON THE JOURNEY

How is God changing me?

I focus on this one thing: Forgetting the past and looking forward to what lies ahead,
I press on to reach the end of the race and receive the heavenly prize for which
God, through Christ Jesus, is calling us.

PHILIPPIANS 3:13-14 NLT

THE ABILITY TO BE FAITHFUL

Not everyone possesses boundless energy or a conspicuous talent. We are not equally blessed with great intellect or physical beauty or emotional strength. But we have all been given the same ability to be faithful.

—Gigi Graham Tchividjian

REFLECTING ON THE JOURNEY

How is God changing me?

His master replied, "Well done, good and faithful servant!
You have been faithful with a few things; I will put you in charge of many things.
Come and share your master's happiness!"

MATTHEW 25:21 NIV

BROKEN AND REDEEMED

The precious truth of Jesus' power as Redeemer is that He has a plan and an ability to progressively restore the broken parts of human experience and to reproduce a whole person.

—Jack Hayford

REFLECTING ON THE JOURNEY

How is God changing me?

All the broken and dislocated pieces of the universe—people and things, animals and atoms—get properly fixed and fit together in vibrant harmonies, all because of His death, His blood that poured down from the Cross.

COLOSSIANS 1:20 THE MESSAGE

Sing to the Lord a new song;

Sing to the Lord, all the earth....

Tell of His glory among the nations,

His wonderful deeds among all the

peoples.... Say among the nations,

"The Lord reigns."

Psalm 96:1, 3, 10 NASB

Among the Nations

The fields, ripe for harvest, are spilling over into our own backyard. While many missionaries are sent to other countries, multitudes of people from those countries meet us face to face here in America.

Although they spent most of their ministry years in another country, Bill and Maggie Farmer now live in the United States. Their goal is still to tell of God's glory among the nations, but now they minister to people from the many cultures He is bringing right into their neighborhood.

When Maggie began teaching an ESL class of ten young women, she felt the Lord impress on her that she should use music to help them with pronunciation. She struggled with the idea since she had been diagnosed with Parkinson's disease and had also undergone a biopsy of her thyroid which left her with a gravelly voice. For years Maggie had loved singing and playing her guitar, taking the gift of music for granted. Now she couldn't depend on either her voice or her right hand.

She prayed about it and hoped God would answer with another teaching strategy. But in the end she had to be willing to swallow her pride and let God use her as He chose.

When she explained her limitations to the young women in the class, they were patient and helpful. One who had beautiful handwriting wrote the words on the board for her. And as they practiced the words of a Scripture song, the girls seemed eager to learn it.

The next week one student walked into class singing the catchy Scripture chorus and commented, "I've been singing that song at home all week." Maggie asked, "Did you know it before?" She answered, "No! You taught it to me last week." The students went on to learn other songs based on God's Word, which will not return to Him void.

Wherever you can, tell of God's glory among the nations. Even—or especially—in your own backyard.

GOD'S STORY

God is writing His story, and He invites us to write it with Him.... We become God's missionary people by joining Christ in the story line of others' lives. And this is the grand narrative that makes sense of life: God is reconciling the world to Himself, and we are invited to join Him.

—Daniel Rickett

REFLECTING ON THE JOURNEY

How is God changing me?

God made my life complete when I placed all the pieces before Him....
God rewrote the text of my life when I opened the book of my heart to His eyes.
PSALM 18:20, 24 THE MESSAGE

SHARE YOUR GRATITUDE

When I look back...I am stirred by the thought of the number of people whom
I have to thank for what they gave me or for what they were to me.

—Albert Schweitzer

REFLECTING ON THE JOURNEY

How is God changing me?

Every time I think of you, I give thanks to my God...for you
have been my partners in spreading the Good News about Christ.
PHILIPPIANS 1:3, 5 NLT

KEEP REACHING OUT

Heavenly Father, speak to me today concerning how to reach out to the world. From the youngest to the oldest, there is something we all can do. Allow me to set an example of compassion and concern for others.... Amen.

—Kim Boyce

REFLECTING ON THE JOURNEY

How is God changing me?

May God be merciful and bless us. May His face smile with favor on us.
May Your ways be known throughout the earth,
Your saving power among people everywhere.

PSALM 67:1-2 NLT

COOPERATE WITH GOD

We have been challenged by the unprecedented opening of doors for evangelism.
Working together, we can seize the opportunities that God keeps placing before us.

REFLECTING ON THE JOURNEY

How is God changing me?

For the earth shall be full of the knowledge of the Lord as the waters cover the sea.
ISAIAH 11:9 NKJV

LIFELONG CALLING

Short-term work, whether two weeks or two years, can indeed be effective and pleasing to God.... It can open participants' eyes to the sometimes gritty realities of the world, make them aware of their own ethnocentrism and of the gifts and courage of non-Western believers, and spark a lifelong commitment to missions.

—Stan Guthrie

REFLECTING ON THE JOURNEY

How is God changing me?

He set it all out before us in Christ, a long-range plan in which
everything would be brought together and summed up in Him,
everything in deepest heaven, everything on planet earth.

EPHESIANS 1:9-10 THE MESSAGE

FIND YOUR ROLE

There is of course a great need for people to go, but there is a greater need for each of us to take up our own responsibility as part of the church's response to the Great Commission; to be personally involved in it whatever our particular role may be.

—George Verwer
Founder, Operation Mobilisation

REFLECTING ON THE JOURNEY

How is God changing me?

Through Him we received both the generous gift of His life and the urgent task of
passing it on to others who receive it by entering into obedient trust in Jesus.

ROMANS 1:5 THE MESSAGE

MY MISSION AT HOME

Most of us who are not "called" to serve as long-term missionaries or self-supporting tentmakers in another country will remain as residents in our homeland. But...the opportunity to participate in world missions at home grows each year as God brings more international people to reside in North America.

—Leiton Chinn
Association of Christians Ministering among Internationals

REFLECTING ON THE JOURNEY

How is God changing me?

He is the great God, the mighty and awesome God, who shows no partiality....
He shows love to the foreigners living among you....
So you, too, must show love to foreigners.
DEUTERONOMY 10:17-19 NLT

Owe no one anything

except to love one another,

for he who loves another

has fulfilled the law.

For the commandments...are

all summed up in this saying, namely,

"You shall love your neighbor

as yourself."

ROMANS 13:8-9 NKJV

Love Your Neighbor

by Mel Cheatham, M.D.

Humanitarian relief worker and advocate, neurosurgeon, and member of the Board of Directors of Samaritan's Purse and the Billy Graham Evangelical Association.

I came to understand this "second" commandment in a never-to-be-forgotten way in October 1993 while doing volunteer work during the war in Bosnia. Our Samaritan's Purse team was working with a Croat Catholic neurosurgeon named Dr. Josip Jurisic.

One afternoon I operated on a Muslim soldier who had been shot in the neck by a sniper's bullet. If he survived, he would remain paralyzed from the neck down and likely be unable to breathe on his own. For this reason, following the operation, the anesthesia tube was left in his airway and connected to a ventilator which was powered by an emergency diesel generator.

The following morning I was making rounds when Dr. Jurisic quietly said, "Professor, do you remember the Muslim soldier you operated on late yesterday? During the night, the supply of diesel fuel ran out. The ventilator stopped working, and he died."

Then he said to me, "The Muslim soldier's friends are vindictive people, and because he died, I fear they will come for you and kill you. Therefore, I have changed the operative record. I have erased your name, and have written my name in place of yours."

Stunned, I looked at Dr. Jurisic for a long moment before stating, "But surely, my friend, this means his Muslim Army friends will come for you and kill you."

Dr. Jurisic replied, "This is not your war. You have come here to help during this time of war, and I am prepared to die in your place if I must, in order that you might live."

What Dr. Jurisic was offering to do for me as his friend came as a powerful reminder of what Jesus did for me and all humanity on the cross. He gave His life that we might live. Because of the Resurrection, He lives today and calls us to love the Lord our God with all our hearts, souls, and minds. Second only to this, He tells us to love our neighbor as we love ourselves.

CALL TO PRAYER

The center of power is not to be found in summit meetings or in peace conferences. It is not in Beijing or Washington or the United Nations, but rather where children of God pray in the power of the Spirit for God's will to be done in their lives, in their homes, and in the world about them.

—Ruth Bell Graham

REFLECTING ON THE JOURNEY

How is God changing me?

My house shall be called a house of prayer for all nations.
ISAIAH 56:7 NKJV

NEARER TO HIM

The spirit of Christ is the spirit of missions. The nearer we get to Him, the more intensely missionary we become.

—Henry Martyn
Missionary to India and Persia

REFLECTING ON THE JOURNEY

How is God changing me?

So let us know, let us press on to know the Lord. His going forth is as certain as the
dawn; and He will come to us like the rain, like the spring rain watering the earth.

HOSEA 6:3 NASB

ANSWERS TO PRAYER

Your prayers move God to change the world. You may not understand the mystery of prayer. You don't need to. But this much is clear: Actions in heaven begin when someone prays on earth. What an amazing thought!

—Max Lucado

REFLECTING ON THE JOURNEY

How is God changing me?

As soon as you began to pray, an answer was given.

DANIEL 9:23 NIV

SERVE WHERE YOU ARE

We are all in missions. Some are called to foreign lands. Some are called to the jungles of the workplace. Wherever you are called, serve the Lord in that place. Let Him demonstrate His power through your life so that others might experience Him through you today.

—Os Hillman
Founder, Marketplace Leaders Ministries

REFLECTING ON THE JOURNEY

How is God changing me?

Why is it that He gives us these special abilities to do certain things best?
It is that God's people will be equipped to do better work for Him,
building up the Church, the body of Christ.

EPHESIANS 4:12 TLB

PROCLAIM HIS NAME

The concern for world evangelization is...rooted in the character of the God who has come to us in Christ Jesus. Thus, it can never be the province of a few enthusiasts, a sideline or a specialty of those who happen to have a bent that way. It is the distinctive mark of being a Christian.

—James S. Stewart

REFLECTING ON THE JOURNEY

How is God changing me?

I have raised you up for this very purpose, that I might show you
My power and that My name might be proclaimed in all the earth.

EXODUS 9:16 NIV

GLOBAL CHRISTIANS

We must be global Christians with a global vision because our God is a global God.

—John Stott

REFLECTING ON THE JOURNEY

How is God changing me?

And this gospel of the kingdom will be preached in all the world
as a witness to all the nations, and then the end will come.

MATTHEW 24:14 NKJV

Christianity does not seek to impose, it proposes. The Gospel is the great proposal: Come to the wedding feast, one and all—black, white, rich, poor, East, West, Muslim, Jew, Christian—all are welcome, and it's never too late. God turns no man or woman away, not one. Through His Son, Jesus Christ, the Father brings us into His Kingdom. This is the promise He holds out to individuals and nations alike...a Kingdom of righteousness, peace, and joy forever in the Holy Spirit.

CHARLES COLSON/HAROLD FICKETT